TAKING TIME
FOR GOD

by Peter Barski

ISBN: 979-8-9873533-0-1

November 1, 2022 Lone Wolf Publishing

https://www.facebook.com/lonewolfpublishing

"But my life is worth nothing unless I use it for doing the work assigned to me by the Lord Jesus – the work of telling others the Good News about God's wonderful kindness and love." Acts 20:24

Introduction

Welcome to the age of technology, where information is but a search engine away. Long gone are the days of collecting Encyclopedia Britannicas and the necessity of rummaging through the library's card catalogs to find long sought after answers to our questions. Enter in Google, where your answer is but a few keystrokes away. And not just one answer, but a whole plethora of answers from multiple sites, often times with varying degrees of accuracy ranging from fact to outright fiction! It certainly takes a discerning person to be able to sift through all the information so easily available to us.

Not only can we research information we may need to find for our school assignments or work, we can also find information about ourselves and the people we are curious about. No longer are our favorite celebrities shrouded in secrecy. The actions of every superstar are spilled onto the internet within minutes, or in many cases, live streamed for our viewing pleasure. All of this instant exposure and popularity has heightened many young people's desire to be noticed, and noticed now. Thus enter in apps such as Twitch and Tiptop. People flock willingly to share their life actions and events on Facebook or Instagram, anything to make them stand out amongst their friends or family and show everyone just how successful and happy they are. But if all of this information about ourselves is so wonderful and elaborate, why is this younger generation so depressed and disconnected? Why has the suicide rate drastically increased amongst younger people and mental health given so much more attention today?

It is not my intention to argue the bad points of today's technology; I leave that to other more capable writers. My goal is to show how technology and the information age has distracted us from spending time with God, the God who loves us dearly and created a lovely planet for us to live on. How can we enjoy the world around us when our minds are focused on the meta verse, an alternate reality? How has Tik-Tok shortened our attention spans, and why has that led to a steep decline in people taking time to read the Bible? Why are people so concerned about what others think about them online instead of what God thinks about them? What are the ways we can reconnect with God? These are the questions I want to address in this book, and hopefully bring some readers back to God and back to reality!

The Shortening Of Our Attention Span

When I was young, I remember when I was assigned a research project for school, a lot of time and effort went into it. It usually required a trip to the library, where I had to find books written about the subject in question. If past newspaper articles had been written on the topic, I had to sift through microfiche. Encyclopedias were a treasure trove of information as well. This process took a long time to be sure. I recall the excited feeling that came over me as I penned together all the supporting facts I had gathered into my final draft. It was a strong feeling of accomplishment that also helped solidify my knowledge of that particular subject matter. When I think of all the time and effort that went into these projects, I can't help but marvel at how much quicker those same projects can be completed today. With the admit of the search engine, gone are the hours of dedicated research required to amass information on a particular subject. A wealth of information is but a few keystrokes away. We are indeed in the middle of the information age.

But with the quickness at which we obtain all this information come with a price? Do we easily become bored? It may sound silly, but it is a valid question. Let me give you a personal example if I may. One afternoon I was watching an older movie with my son. One of the lead characters was John Voight, and I mentioned that he still looked the same now as he did back then, at least in his facial features. My son replied that he thought his daughter, Angelina Jolie looked a little like him in the face. Now I had no idea that Angelina Jolie was his daughter, and that sparked my curiosity. So I took out my i- phone and searched on Google to find out if that was true or not. In less than ten seconds I affirmed that my son was indeed correct. I thought to myself, "well that was interesting, I didn't know that," and then went on watching the movie. Even though I had retained that tiny bit of information, it was the ease of obtaining it that quickly led me to move on from the subject. My attention quickly shifted back to the movie and the day went on as normal. There was no necessity to research it any further and I soon forgot about it. But that is my point, with less effort comes a certain lackadaisical attitude if you please. We are so used to getting what we want so quickly and effortlessly that we have become apathetic.

Here is another example of the changes led by technology and the internet. Do you know anyone who keeps photo albums? If you do, are they below the age of thirty? Time was, a person took pictures of a special event with a camera. Then they had to go to the store to get the pictures developed. A few days later, that person excitedly rummaged through the photos recalling the fun time they had. Some people would take the time to make photo albums of their children, close family and vacations. It was a time consuming endeavor, but fun. One was always eager to share these photos with guests or extended family members. It was a time of sharing, not only photos, but the stories behind them. Now of course, all one has to do is post a photo from their phone onto whichever social platform they wish. Not only is it quick and easy, it is free. Long gone are the days of camera film and developing, enter in the age of convenience.

But I think the best examples of how our attention spans are diminishing are in the increased popularity of the apps Tik-Tok and WeChat. Both have an endless array of short video loops on them to watch that usually last shorter of thirty seconds. Tik-Tok being more popular with the younger generation, it is quite something to see a person flip through these endless streams of short "clips" all the while with their head "buried into their phone." If something catches their interest, they watch the clip to the end and perhaps make a comment or like the video. If they do not find it interesting, they simply flip (skip forward) to the next video. A person has the ability to watch hundreds, if not thousands of clips per day, and the content is endless. Do you honestly think that a younger person who watches so many short video clips in such a short time will have the patience to sit down and read a book? I don't think so, and yet these are the things that parents have to contend with today. Is it possible parents can limit their children's time on their phones? Yes, but is it plausible? What about the adult reading this book, do you find yourself spending too much time on your phone and not enough time spending it with God? What are some changes you can make to rectify that situation? Before we answer that, let us take a look at some other distractions popping up in our world courtesy of technology.

Alternate Reality

Have you ever travelled on a subway train during a weekday rush hour commute? Noticed how everyone is staring down at their phones? Perhaps they are catching up on the news or looking at their Facebook feed. The thing to note is that each individual is in their own little "bubble" so to speak, where they do not want to be disturbed by anyone around them. Perhaps they feel safe in their own little bubble, but noteworthy is that no one is socializing. There is no communicating with other people, and I dare say that if you tried to start a conversation with anyone while they are in their bubble, you would be met with a glance of annoyance.

Let me give you another example. Have you ever gone to a restaurant and seen a group of people sitting at a table, each one of them looking down at their phone? Perhaps they are work associates or a group of friends, but sadder still is if it is a family. Instead of engaging each other in conversation, they are too busy spending time on their phones. Perhaps they are taking pictures of their food in order to post on Instagram, or they are tagging their location on Facebook in order to show off to their "friends" where they are at. But as for enjoying the company they are with at that present moment, nonexistent.

It is this desire to be active on this online, alternate reality that is so disconcerting. Now, it seems, something taking over people's attention from the real world is the "meta verse." Already there are multiple platforms you can choose from to partake in these alternate universes including HyperNation, Roblox and even Facebook, which has now been renamed Meta. On these various platforms people can build things and even join real life celebrities such as Snoop Dogg for parties or raves. Mark Zuckerburg has invested billions of dollars to research how to make the metaverse as realistic as possible, hoping to provide a memorable online experience.

Needless to say is that this all takes us away from the real world we are living in, a beautiful world with interesting people living all around us. These online apps and platforms supposedly put us in a happier, more fun place. They create a distraction, if you will, from everyday life. But if people are really so much happier on these social networks and metaverse platforms, why are teens and young adults suffering from depression and anxiety at such record numbers?

An Unhappy Generation

Studies and research have revealed that depression and anxiety in teens and young adults are at record levels. A whole range of reasons have been given for this occurrence. It has been suggested that the pandemic has caused stress amongst the younger kids, but studies showed that depression and anxiety were steadily rising well before Covid-19 hit. Perhaps more relevant are the pressures that social media apps bring to our children.

In an age when everyone is posting all the fun activities they are partaking in, it can cast an unrealistic expectation on young people. All they see are the numerous posts of different friends travelling to the Bahamas for a holiday away, or off to the Rockies for a ski trip. They begin to wonder why their family never goes away on fun, extravagant trips. They don't realize that the vast majority of their peers are of the working class sort and also don't go to these fun destinations. All they are exposed to is the constant barrage of happy people living extravagant lifestyles. I call it "deceiver's remorse," in that these social media apps deceive them into believing that this is the norm for everyday people, and not the extreme. Most families have to save up for years in order to take a family vacation somewhere, but since most people do not post about every day, boring life, a person is only exposed to the fun activities that their "friends" online post about. I dare say they are bludgeoned with these posts, thereby giving them an exaggerated expectation of how life should be lived, and they ultimately become depressed by their own dull and remorseful lives.

But perhaps they do find occasion to post something interesting about themselves online. There is also the system of likes and dislikes, and also the number of views one gets on their video posts. A measure of one's success is kept track by the number of likes or views they get. This is most apparent on Instagram. People aim to get as many likes as they can by gaining large numbers of followers. The more followers one has, the better their chances are for getting numerous likes for whatever photos they post onto their online account. It sounds trivial, but it is hard to argue the fact that some people have made a "success" of themselves by gaining millions of followers. They are deemed "influencers" by the powers that be and are paid enormous sums of money by companies to model their clothing, or wear their sunglasses or use their products. This also is a false deception to the everyday youngster who feels that anyone can obtain this "influencer" status, when in reality it only happens to a very small percentage of people online. These youngsters are starving for online attention and may even begin to post pictures of themselves wearing skimpy bikinis to attract a larger following online. They fervently check how many likes they have received on a post they just uploaded and oftentimes become depressed when they can't seem to reach their goal, however unrealistic that may be.

Kids are constantly bombarded with social media and the measurements of success online. They find themselves anxious to upload that next "viral" video of themselves, and of course when that doesn't happen, become depressed with a feeling of worthlessness. "What is it that makes a person popular online," they ask themselves. "What can I do to make myself more noticeable?"

Ultimately, though, I believe the true cause of all this loneliness, despair and anxiety people feel is from their lack of contact with God. Can hours and hours of scrolling through Tik- Tok videos bring a person true happiness? I don't think so, but when a person observes their surroundings, all you can see are people glued to their phones.

Certainly to be entertained has always been a propensity of humans, and the evolution of technology has certainly made it so much more easier for us to be. But in some regard, it has made us so much more separated from our surroundings, and from God. This has ultimately led us to become a much more sadder generation than that of our predecessors. But it is never too late to find true happiness.

Happiness Through God

How many people do you know who have read the Bible in its entirety? "Who has time?" is a common reply when asking someone if they have. And yet it is, in my opinion, a vital necessity for getting to know God and His characteristics. One evening while discussing God's character with someone, they described Him as "a harsh taskmaster who keeps track of every sin we commit." But if a person were to read the Bible completely through, they would see God in a completely different light.

I admit I had ideas of a God that was a strict record keeper, making note of all my faults. I had even read the majority of the New Testament, albeit sporadically and not in any particular order. It wasn't until I found myself at a rock bottom in my life that I began to read the Bible from beginning to end. I was unemployed at the time and the country was in lockdown due to the Covid-19 epidemic, so I did have a lot of spare time to read. But something drew me to it, and I am forever grateful for that. I read about a God that was loving and forgiving, not a God that was strict and taxing. I found out about a God who is patient and not quick to anger. What amazed me the most was how the Old Testament revealed how much God wanted us to turn to Him, blessing the people of Israel when they did so.

The important point to make is by taking the time to read the Bible, I came to know God much better. It is so easy to get caught up in the cares of this world and the routine of everyday life that we lose sight of the fact that this planet was made for us by a loving God who wants us to seek His guidance in everything we do. He is our Father, if only we would come to realize that and listen to Him. By wanting to please God instead of the people around us or our "followers" on the internet, life would take on a whole new wonderful meaning. Unfortunately those who truly seek out God and long to do what is pleasing to Him are few and far between. Jesus commented about this over two thousand years ago when the disciples asked why the whole world could not receive the Holy Spirit, and He replied: "Because the world is not looking for it." John 14:17 Oh how true it was then, and how much more so today, each of us in our own little "bubble," on our gadgets or laptops, occupied with whatever distraction it can offer us.

Just imagine a world of people seeking out God, our Creator. What would that look like? It all started with one person, Abraham in the Old Testament. Why was he known as a man of faith? Well think about the world he lived in at the time. There was no internet, not even electricity, but more importantly was the fact that there was no Bible back then. Think about how strong his belief was in a God that existed to provide for him, a God he had not seen nor read of, yet he put all his faith in this God, and how blessed he became, becoming the "father" of a nation.

Let me ask you dear reader a straight forward question, do you believe in God? If you answered "yes," then wouldn't you want to do everything in your power to build that "seed of faith" into a flourishing "tree of faith," one that is rooted deep in the knowledge of God? I believe the best way to accomplish that is to read the entire Bible, starting with Genesis. I recommend a study Bible that has notes (explanations) on many of the verses. I have the Life Application Study Bible that I have found most appropriate, with pertinent details about certain sections and verses that I would not have known on my own. The point is to take time and read it. We may not have another pandemic in our lifetimes to shut down the world economy, thus giving us extra time on our hands, but a sincere heart that is anxious to get to know God better will dedicate the time needed to read God's Word.

Now some people may say that reading the Old Testament is a waste of time and that it does not pertain to them, but I feel that is incorrect. By reading the Old Testament we learn of God's characteristics, which reflect love, patience and purity. Many may be surprised to learn that there are many references to Jesus' future coming in the Old Testament, with some of those verses written hundreds of years before He did.

Now I am no theologian, nor am I a scholar, but in my studies of the Bible, it seems to me that the Jewish people were given the first opportunity for Christ's salvation because of Abraham's faith long ago. What I mean is that as the generations passed, people began to worship hand carved deities or celestial bodies, but Abraham worshiped the one true God, Jehovah. And because of his faith, Jesus was born from the Jewish lineage, preaching to the Jews about the good news of God's love and salvation. That is what was meant when Jesus said "salvation came through the Jews." John 4:22 Of course God loves all people, but because of Abraham's faith long ago, Israel was given the first opportunity to experience Jesus' miracles and learn from Him first hand. I do not in any way believe that the gentiles were considered second rate citizens by

God, and that it was His divine plan for people the world over to experience His love through Jesus' death on the cross. And what love it is!

"But how can I experience God's love?" you may ask. My answer is to take time for God. Put away those "worries of the world," so to speak, and come to know God. Begin right now by praying to Jesus, asking Him to forgive you of all your past sins. Talk to Jesus with a sincere heart, for God knows our hearts. Tell Him that you want to know God better and experience the joy of calling Him your Father. Do you have a longing to experience His love and compassion? Make time for God and see how much your life can change!

God Our Father

Do you think of God as someone who never forgets our wrong doings; someone who keeps a record of all our sins and wrong doings? Do you feel that God is out to punish you for being a sinner, for not being perfect? My suggestion is to come and know God better.

When I read the Old Testament, I read about a God who created a beautiful planet for us and who loves us as a heavenly Father, being extremely patient and merciful. Jesus revealed this name to us numerous times, calling God our Father (and also His), and us being His children. What a wonderful name for God: our Heavenly Father. And as for us, we are His children. What a beautiful revelation! But it seems as human beings progress over time in their intelligence, they become more independent, substituting their reliance on God for learned knowledge. But even with all our advances in science and medicine, we suffer from depression and anxiety in alarming numbers. Why is that?

Jesus told us that Heaven belongs to the childlike. Matthew 18:2 If we would only trust God as a child trusts their earthly parents, how much more rewarding life would be for us! It is that utter and complete faith that we put in our parents to provide and care for us, without worrying about where tomorrow's dinner will come from, that we need to put into God, our Heavenly Father. Jesus even told us: "being of evil hearts, when our children ask for bread, would we give them a stone instead? How much more would your Heavenly Father provide for you if you but ask and believe?" Matthew 7:11

Perhaps you may want to point out that there are parents who have neglected, abused and even starved their children. But that points even more so to the purity and graciousness of our Heavenly Father, who wants to provide for us if we would but ask and believe. Our Heavenly Father is pure love and completely contrasts the evil things that people do on earth. Jesus, understanding this, pointed it out in Matthew 7:11, but all we concentrate on is the terrible and abhorrent things we see and hear on the news. No wonder younger people are turning to apps and alternate realities to escape these images of sadness. We as a population need to get back to basics, so to speak. We need to watch a little less television and read a lot more of the Bible. We should rely less on ourselves and trust God a whole lot more.

This may take some time for someone to let go of their anxieties and worries and trust God completely, I know it did for me. Especially in a world where people are always on the go and expected to work hard in order to provide for themselves and their loved ones, it can be easy to lose focus. But as I learned about God's loving characteristics and earnestly prayed with a sincere heart, I found a God that provided and still provides for my needs, a God that has not let me down. And with that trust that builds over time comes the relinquishment of all my anxieties and fears. Worries evaporate and a whole new feeling of comfort is instilled. This becomes evident by the people who know me, especially people who knew me before I was saved, and they are amazed by the change they see in me. No longer do I stress over matters that I once worried so much about. I am not here to say that all the storms in life will cease, troubles come, but I lay them down before God in prayer and trust in Him to pull me through whatever situation may arise.

What if you come across someone who points out all the laws God passed down to the people of Moses' day? "How strict and taxing God seems in those passages." Rubbish! Did the people back then have any awareness of viruses or bacterial infections? Of course not; microscopes had not even been invented. What about knowledge of high cholesterol or the foods that can elevate lipid levels, do you think they had any knowledge of that? That is why God mandated that a person quarantine when they contracted an infectious skin disease or that they not eat certain foods. Do you think it was by chance that God instructed them to eat only fish with fins and scales but not seafood such as shrimp or lobster? As tasty as shrimp and lobster are, they are also much higher in cholesterol than fish, thereby making them less healthier to eat. To me this points to not only an all loving and caring God, but also an all knowledgeable one. A God, being our Heavenly Father, setting boundaries for our own good because He cares for us immensely.

Of course Jesus told us that it did not matter what we ate, that food would not defile us. It is what is inside a person's heart that matters. Mark 7:14-23 He was talking about inner purity and what our hearts longed for that was important. Maintaining a strict diet will not bring us closer to God. It may help prolong our lives physically, but spiritually speaking, it cannot save us.

Does your heart long for acceptance and love? I assure you that you cannot find that in the metaverse. Take time to learn about the goodness of God and His immeasurable love for you. Seek God and take time to know Him instead of seeking the things that the world offers, because in the end, it is all just pointless. The only thing that will matter is your relationship with God through His son Jesus.

God's Patience And Love

Many people have the misperception that God is watching over them, ready to punish them for every "misstep" they take. But I have read of a patient God, one who loves us and is quick to forgive. I am not saying there are no consequences to our sins, for I know firsthand that there are. But by correcting us, as a good Father would do, He brings us back to Him, and how wonderful that is. Think of it as God "guiding" us through our everyday lives. For to not need His guidance, we would have to be perfect individuals, and of course none of us are. To call upon God for His good Grace and guidance is exactly what He wants us to do. When we stray from God's ways, unknowingly or knowingly, consequences will naturally arise. It can affect other people, but most often it affects us. The first thing we should do is recognize what it was we did wrong, and then immediately ask Jesus to forgive us of our wrongdoings (sins), making us acceptable again to God. Stopping the sinful acts altogether (repentance) can be a struggle for us, but by sincerely wanting to stop and most importantly, asking God to help us, we can turn away from those sinful acts that are so tempting to us.

God also wants us to ask Him for our needs and to depend upon Him to provide them. By doing this we eliminate all anxieties and worries. Of course we need to feel those necessities in our lives, hence the "storms" that we come across, for how can we experience comfort if we have no need for it? One must experience that need for comfort in order to desire it. That is where faith and patience comes in. We must believe that God will provide for us and then be patient, just as he is patient with us. Oh but how rewarding it is when we see our prayers answered! It helps to solidify our faith in God, as long as what we ask for is in line with God's will. To ask God for us to win the lottery is a want, not a need, but to ask God to provide us with food to feed our family is a need.

And why shouldn't we be patient while waiting for our prayers to be answered? God is certainly patient with us. Over and over the Bible points out God's patience when dealing with us, it is incredible to read about. For example, when God had seen how wicked people had become and decided to flood the earth, He instructed Noah to build an ark. During this time of building it gave the people over one hundred years to repent and turn to God. Unfortunately they did not, and the vast majority of mankind was wiped out. But to think of that time frame leading up to the flood, essentially a person's lifetime, it certainly shows how patient God is in dealing with us. Jesus mentioned this in Matthew Chapter 24 when He said that "as the days of Noah were, so shall also the coming of the Son of man be. For as in the days that were before the flood they were eating and drinking…..until the day that Noah entered into the ark." Don't be caught by surprise dear reader, as the people back in that day were. Turn to Jesus and God, for we cannot say we weren't warned.

Time after time I read of God's patience with His people, sending prophets instructing them to turn from their evil and misguided ways. These prophets also conveyed God's love for them as well. It seems that the past prophets were speaking to us as well. For example, in Isaiah chapter seven, the birth of Jesus was foretold: "The virgin will conceive a child! She will give birth to a son and will call him Immanuel – 'God is with us.'" This was written about seven hundred years before Jesus was born. Then in chapter thirty Isaiah offers us hope in God: "But the Lord still waits for you to come to Him so He can show you His love and compassion. For the

Lord is a faithful God. Blessed are those who wait for Him to help them. He will be gracious if you ask for help." What a pertinent statement made so long ago for the people then and for us now! Notice the words used here: love, compassion, faithful and gracious. I certainly see a God that is full of love and patience for us, if we would just take the time to notice.

One of the most famous verses in the Bible shouts out to us of this love, John 3:16: "For God so loved the world that He gave His one and only Son, that whoever believes in Him shall not perish but have eternal life." But even throughout the Old Testament words of love ring loudly to us. God said to them in the book of Hosea, "I do not want your sacrifices, I want your love; I don't want your offerings – I want you to know me." So even before God sent Jesus to die on the cross so our sins could be forgiven and we could be made acceptable to God, He said He just wanted us to know Him. But how are we to know Him if we don't take the time to do so? To start we can put away those distracting devices and gadgets so to speak. Please dear reader, come to know a loving and patient God, a God that wants to bless you and provide for you. Personally I would rather gain the love of God than a million likes on my Instagram page!

God Our Good Shepherd

Can you imagine what a shepherd looks like in your mind? Picture someone carrying a staff while diligently watching over their flock of sheep, keeping them safe and protecting them from harm. But have you ever thought of God as being your shepherd? God wants to provide for you and protect you. He wants to feed you when you are hungry and provide you shelter from the storms of life, but today people needlessly worry about these things themselves instead of placing their concerns before God. It amazes me how stressed people are over their ability to provide a home and food for themselves and their loved ones, basic necessities that God knows we need. Yes there are lots of successful people out there who devote all their time and effort into becoming rich, but as Jesus said, "for what good is it for a man to gain the whole world and lose his own soul?" Matthew 16:26 But I am not talking about being a successful millionaire, I am talking about abandoning all fears and anxieties.

The Bible states that God is our good shepherd, both in the Old and New Testaments. In Isaiah chapter forty it states: "Like a shepherd He will tend His flock." Then in John chapter ten Jesus states that He is the good shepherd that lays down his life for the sheep. Again, what does a shepherd do? He protects his flock from harm, he feeds them and he watches over them. By trusting Jesus and God with your necessities, it allows you to shed all concerns and worries about these things. It is such a simple concept that it sounds almost too easy to be true, but it is. Of course being human, we have to complicate things, adding to them unnecessary burdens.

Consider if you will a sheep that was frail and sickly. A sheep who even though had a shepherd standing alongside it, ready to provide food and comfort, decided to "go it alone" so to speak. Perhaps this sheep said to itself, "I am aware of this good shepherd beside me, who is willing to take care of me, but I don't deserve His help, I am a lowly sheep unworthy of His provision." Or perhaps the sheep feels that it must provide for itself, even though there is a shepherd willing and able to care for it. It only trusts itself to take care of it, not the shepherd. How silly this all sounds, but that is exactly what we do. Even though it is spelled out as clear as day in the Bible that God is our good Shepherd, we stress and worry over things that we shouldn't. But being the "intelligent" humans that we are, we add all of these "buts" and "ifs," and in the process complicate a simple concept, bringing on a whole slew of worries and anxieties that are really needless in our lives.

It is important here to distinguish between wants and needs. Many people want to be a millionaire, but do you truly need a million dollars? Jesus was very clear about a rich person's chance of entering Heaven. He said, "It is easier for a camel to fit through the eye of a needle than it is for a rich man to enter Heaven." Matthew 19:24 This makes me wonder how these rich pastors and televangelists can justify their riches, but I transgress. What I am speaking of is our needs in life for survival. "Which of you, if your son asks for bread, will give him a stone....and if you then, though you are evil, know how to give good gifts to your children, how much more will your Father in Heaven give good gifts to those who ask Him!" Matthew 7: 9-11 God, your Heavenly Father, your good Shepherd, wants to provide for you, if you would only ask and believe.

I have to admit, I struggled with this concept of believing God will provide for me for some time. Whenever life threw me a curveball: a job opportunity lost, or a paycheck delayed, boy did I sweat it. But with each unexpected hurdle, God came through for me every time. What have I learned? God is my good Shepherd and wants to feed and provide for me. He wants to lead me down green pastures and tend to me. The issue is trusting God utterly and completely. That is where faith comes in. As time goes by and I see God's handiwork in my life, my faith has become stronger and stronger, and my worrying less and less. It is a wonderful feeling that almost seems to go against the rational thinking of today's society. "Look at the birds of the air; they do not sow or reap or store away in barns, and yet your Heavenly Father feeds them. Are you not much more valuable than they? Can any one of you by worrying add a single hour to your life?" Matthew 6: 26-27   Oh what joy fills my heart as I pen these words to paper! If only everyone could experience God's love and comfort, what happier "sheep" we would be.

Of course I do not mean for us to sit back in our easy chair and wait lazily for God to provide for us. That is just folly. If you find yourself unemployed or in need, the first thing you should do is bring your needs to God in prayer. Then prudently, not hastily, go and search for an appropriate job. I knew a pharmacist who found himself suddenly out of a job once. He printed up copies of his resume and then proceeded to drive around to his local pharmacies in the area handing out his resume until he found a store owner that needed help. Perhaps jumping online to search Indeed or Glassdoor will help you find an employer in need of your skills. God will make it happen for you if you but ask and believe. It is His good pleasure to provide for His flock. The important thing is to ask and have faith.

Perhaps someone you know may ask, "Why are you so calm under such circumstances? I would be panicking right now!" What a glorious response to say, "Because I know God will provide for me." It would be a true testimony to God's love and care for you to say that with true confidence. And if you are met with this response, "What makes you so deserving of God's provisions?" you can say "Because I believe in Jesus and He told me so!" Of course we are not perfect. We are sinners and falter in our humanly ways, but by praying to Jesus, asking for His forgiveness, we are indeed forgiven. It is that letting go of our past that can hinder us at times, and that leads us into the next chapter.

Letting Go Of The Past

Picture for a moment a young man in his twenties or thirties who decides to go off and hike into the woods for a weekend. He wants to see if he can survive on his own and therefore packs no food provisions, bringing with him only his tent, fishing pole and odd supplies he feels is necessary. He spends most of the day Friday hiking, wanting to get as far away from civilization as possible, admiring the beauty of the forest and all of the wildlife he sees along the way. Eventually he hikes upon a stream and decides that it is a good place to make camp. The sound of the water flowing feels tranquil to him and he can fish for food there as well. It takes him longer to get his tent set up than he expected and so he does not have time to catch himself dinner that evening, and feeling a little weary from the long hike, he decides to get to sleep so he can get an early start of things in the morning.

The next day he wakes up very hungry and is motivated to go catch some fish. He walks up stream quite a ways until he finds an area that is deep enough to fish. Having seen what looks to be a swirl of water created by a fish tail, he wades into the stream a bit to get closer. Unfortunately the rocks in the water bed are rather slippery, and he loses his footing. As he falls, he loses his grip of the fishing pole. The water is much deeper than he realizes and he has to struggle hard to stay afloat as the stream is flowing strongly. After getting drenched by the cold water and frantically swimming to shore, he realizes that he had his only lighter in his pocket, which is now lost in the river somewhere. Not only that, his fishing pole was nowhere to be found, confounding his situation. After catching his breath he laughs to himself thinking about this bad twist of fate. "Perhaps I am not as much of an outdoorsman as I thought!"

Not wanting to get too discouraged, he treks back to his campsite and begins to shape a stick into a sharp object in order to catch some food, whether it be a fish or some small wildlife like a rabbit. Unfortunately he is shivering from wearing wet clothes, and with no way to make a fire, only gets colder by the minute. It isn't long before he punctures his hand with the knife and is wounded. He uses his shirt as a bandage, wrapping it around his hand to stop the bleeding. He decides to get undressed and calls it a day, hanging his clothes out to dry and bundling up in his sleeping bag for warmth.

That night he wakes up with a fever and chills. He realizes that nature has gotten the best of him and decides to pack up and leave in the morning. But much to his dismay, when morning comes it begins to deluge rain. Aching and feverish, he waits for the rain to stop. By the time he gets started hiking back through the woods it is late Sunday afternoon. Being feverish, he soon loses his bearing and gets lost. It is not until midnight that he finds a road to walk alongside of.

Desperately in need of some help, he finds hope when a truck approaches him. He frantically waves and the driver stops. "Can I please get a ride into town?" he asks the kind older man. "Of course, hop in the back of the truck." Wearily our young man climbs into the bed of the truck and sits down. Before starting off the old man asks, "Aren't you going to take your heavy backpack off?" Our beleaguered young man replies, "You have been so kind as to give me a ride, I couldn't possibly take anymore advantage of your kindness than I already have."

Sound strangely silly? But that is exactly what many people do once they ask Jesus to forgive them of all their sins. Weary from a long, tiresome struggle of life without God, they come to Jesus, dejected, anxious or afraid. They pour out their heart to Jesus and ask for forgiveness, then they carry around their past with them, saying to themselves, "I am too unworthy of God's blessings and love." They totally miss the fact that their past is forgiven and forgotten.

It is important to know that your past does not define who you are. It may have shaped you into the person you are today, but God uses our past for good purposes. It becomes an opportunity for you to reach out to people who are struggling with things you used to. A former drug addict can now become a sponsor or work at a rehabilitation facility. Perhaps they can even become a prison outreach minister. You can be a true blessing in someone else's life that needs to hear your story. It is a way to connect with those in need.

To come to Jesus and ask for forgiveness, giving our lives to Him to shape and mold, yet be afraid to ask God to bless us with our needs because we feel unworthy is silly. It is just like our young friend who would not take off his heavy backpack just because he thought it was too much to ask from a man who had stopped to give him a ride. It is just plain silly. Yet so many people do that very thing!

It is God's good pleasure to provide for His children, and that is exactly what we become when we ask Jesus to forgive us of all our sins. Not some of our sins, but all of them. Jesus eliminates our past sins, and once our sins are wiped away, it makes us acceptable to God, who loves and cares for us dearly. That is why He is called our Heavenly Father, because He cares and provides for us, just like our earthly fathers did, but even more so. There is no reason for us, once we have prayed to Jesus to forgive us, to carry around the sins of our past. It is burdensome and it hinders us. We should approach God in reverent confidence, knowing He loves us and wants us to be comforted.

Of course I am not saying there are no repercussions to our sins. There are consequences that can affect us and also other people, whether that would be family members or others in our lives. A former drug addict may find that they now have hepatitis or HIV, but that in no way disqualifies them from praying to God. Your past does not enslave you. In Romans 8:15 it says: "So you should not be like cowering, fearful slaves. You should behave instead like God's very own children, adopted into His family, calling Him 'Father, dear Father.'" What a beautiful verse! To be able to call God, the creator of all things, our Father is a wonderful privilege. It should take away all anxieties and fears, knowing that the God of Heaven and earth is now your Father, your provider.

It is that letting go of the past that seems to hinder so many people. Won't you take a moment if you haven't already, or if you are unsure if you have, to ask Jesus to forgive you of ALL of your sins, both past and present, thereby making you acceptable to God? What a wonderful revelation to know that you are now a child of God, and as such, can reverently approach Him in prayer. Thank you Jesus and thank you God.

Where Do I Start?

If you are wondering around in the forest of life, encountering setbacks or feeling a sense of confusion about where you are in life, may I suggest you take some time and get to know God. The very first thing to do is to pray, with a sincere and honest heart to Jesus. Ask Him to forgive you of all your sins and impure thoughts so that you may become a child of God. Stop struggling to find acceptance in meaningless social apps. In fact, stop all of your struggling and give your concerns and worries, anxieties and fears to God. For me I did that at a time when I had hit an absolute "rock bottom" in my life, with nowhere to turn and no one to turn to, not even family. Fortunately you don't have to wait for that scenario to happen, but it does entail a sort of "letting go" and "letting God" take over your circumstances and your life. It's a complete abandoning of not yourself, but your will to control things in your life. It is a complete and utterly unflinching faith in God to direct your path that is critical. Abraham exhibited that kind of faith and was blessed to become the father of the nation of Israel because of it.

I would then recommend purchasing a study Bible to start reading. I have a New Living Translation Holy Study Bible that is easy to read and has footnotes, maps and charts that help explain certain verses of the Bible. I would then begin reading from the first book in the Old Testament, Genesis, and proceed forward from there. Remember, no one can read the Bible in a day, so don't get discouraged by how slowly you are progressing. Even in the height of the pandemic and being unemployed at the time, it still took me six months to read the entire Old Testament. But I assure you, it will be worth it, learning about God and His love for all people who truly seek Him.

When you reach the New Testament, you will see God incarnate in Jesus. The Jewish people of that time were expecting a worldly king who would deliver them from the oppressing empires of the world. They were not expecting Jesus, who in His own words said, "I did not come to judge the world, but to save it." John 3:17 His teachings revealed to us love and mercy and compassion, while He also told us of a Heavenly Father that cared for and loved us. Jesus did deliver us from an oppressor, and that was death from sin. When He died on the cross and His blood was shed, it allowed all people the opportunity to become children of God by praying for His forgiveness. What a beautiful sacrifice, for Him to lay down His life so that we could live ours. There is not greater love.

Once you begin to read God's word, take time to notice the beautiful planet we live on. I am fortunate enough to live in a neighborhood that is a bird sanctuary, and now I enjoy drinking my morning cup of coffee sitting outside and watching the many species of birds fly overhead. If you live in the city, try traveling to the local park to watch a sunset. Turn off that television set or radio and watch a sunrise more often. It really is peaceful to see and helps sooth the soul. When driving to work, leave you radio off and enjoy some quiet time with God. When I see rays of sunlight beaming through a large cloud while driving, I think of God and His beauty shining through all of the darkness around me.

Don't be afraid to talk to Jesus and God. Tell Him your feelings. Perhaps you are upset or disappointed that you didn't get that job you applied for. Tell Him about it. Perhaps you are feeling impatient and really want to start a relationship with someone. Tell Him about it. Tell Him your needs. Perhaps your car broke down and you don't have enough money to get it fixed, or worse yet, you lost your home to a hurricane or flood. Pray to God to provide for you. He is there to help and comfort you, especially since you now trust Him and have become a child of God. Have faith and patience and watch as God answers your prayers. Remember that God is Spirit John 4:24 and is looking for those who pray to Him that way, in a sincere and trusting manner.

Inversely, don't be afraid to listen to God as well. Perhaps it is a lyric to a song that encourages you, or even something a person says to you. I remember taking a job with a roofing company because I could not work in the pharmacy profession at the time. I worked alongside the owner for a couple of days learning and then was put out on my own, but he did not like the pace I worked at. One day he asked me what I had done previously, and I said I was in the medical profession most of my life. He replied, "Perhaps you should stay in the medical profession." Now it would have been easy for me to get upset with him for making such a remark, but he was right. Soon enough I was able to get back into the medical field and do what I truly enjoy doing. I just had to listen and trust in God's timing.

If you are looking for a long term relationship with that special someone, listen to what they say when you meet someone new. If you meet a person on a date and they seem absolutely "dreamy," but they smoke cigarettes or talk about using drugs, take that as a sign that they are not the right one for you. What are that person's priorities? If they are contrary to what you feel is God's ways, then move on. If you are unsure, pray to God about it. Ask Him for guidance. Remember that a person's body is God's temple for His Spirit to live in, so if a person uses drugs or smokes cigarettes or drinks in excess, then chances are excellent that God's Spirit does not reside within them. So avoid relationships with people who do those kinds of things, for how can you have a relationship blessed by God if they are ungodly?

Be open for growth by walking with God every day, and as your prayers are answered, you will grow in your faith. Some people expect some grand religious feeling or transformation to take place once they accept Jesus or get baptized, but I personally have not encountered that. What I have experienced is a growth, slow and steady, that has helped to solidify my faith. Changes take place in one's life that may be subtle but reveal God's Spirit working within you. For example, I grew up with a love for rock and prog music. I admired the musicianship of such bands as Rush and Yes. But once

I started reading the Bible, and later getting baptized, I stopped listening to that kind of music. I now enjoy the uplifting music I hear on Christian radio instead. It's the subtle changes over time that helps others to see the wonderful work that God has done in your life, which helps to testify to His love and grace.

Your Faith and God's Grace

When I say that my faith has grown, I do not mean by doing good deeds or stopping bad habits. Those things are a byproduct of faith through time. My faith grew as I read the Bible and learned about God and His characteristics. By God's grace my eyes were opened and I saw just how much He loves us. As time went by I saw not only how God provided for me, but how His timing was perfect in every situation that arose in my times of need. I began to trust God more and more, and it was by trusting God that I grew in my faith, seeing my prayers answered and my needs provided for, sometimes in such harrowing times that some people would have deemed it impossible to happen or useless to try. It is the virtue of patience that was and still is at times the most difficult to institute. When a prayer was not answered in the time frame I would have liked it to have been answered, I had to remind myself that God was and is in control, and if it was not meant to happen, then it was for my own good. Of course once a prayer was answered, I was able to see how perfect God's timing was. And for me that is how my faith and God's grace are interlocked so to speak. By God's good grace I am now able to call Him my Father and rely on Him completely to provide all of my needs.

Let me reiterate to you that it is not by any good act or deed that I am accepted by God, it is only through His good grace that I am saved. By believing that God sent His only son Jesus into the world to die for our sins and praying to Jesus to forgive me of all my sins, I am transformed into a life unencumbered by my past mistakes. Nothing I do or say will make me redeemed; it is only by the grace of God that I am who I am today. Yes I still struggle with sin and sinful desires (humanity) but I have learned to take these urgencies in prayer and ask Jesus for forgiveness. I also ask God for the fortitude to resist them and the patience to deal with something that I may be struggling with.

It is relying on God, and not myself, that is such a saving grace. There is something refreshing about knowing you have God on your side that allows you to be free of all anxieties over the future. It is that knowledge of being accepted by Him that makes you happy in this life. Of course it took some time for me to reach the level of trust I have in God now, and I find myself still growing each and every day, but it is a wonderful feeling once you are cognizant of it.

Taking the time to learn about God and His love for us was the best thing to ever happen to me. I feel excited to share this with others in the best way I know how, and that is through writing. I have always been better at conveying my feelings on paper than by speaking, and if I can reach just one reader, then I would feel extremely joyful and happy. And that is my hope for you, to feel the same way. Stop searching for acceptance on social media apps. Stop getting distracted by pointless notifications. Instead, concentrate on the love God has for you and turn to Jesus to help you get the most out of this life you have been given.

If you are experience anxiety or depression and cannot seem to find the acceptance you long for online, may I suggest you take some time to get to know God. Ask Jesus to forgive you of all your sins and help you to learn about God. It is not something that is required of you to do in public. In fact Jesus encouraged people to pray in private. Matthew 6: 5-8 If you feel unsure about something, reach out to a local church for guidance, but the best guidance is found right inside the Bible. Pray about your worries and concerns, give them up to Jesus, for He is your good Shepherd who can walk you out into greener pastures. God wants you to be comforted and provided for.

Are you wondering around in the woods of this dark world, alone, stumbling and getting hurt? Are you close to hitting rock bottom, contemplating suicide? Are you caught up in a ravaging drug addiction that has cost you everything? Perhaps your marriage is on the verge of breaking and you don't know where to turn. I am here to tell you that it is never too late, anything is possible with God! And what's more, He wants the best for you. He is the God of all comfort. Come and experience God's grace, drink from the well that provides living water and be comforted. God accepts you even with all your faults and is eager for you to experience His love. Put down that phone and spend time with God, it is the best thing you could ever do.

If you are ready, go somewhere quiet and pray this prayer. Let go of the past that has dragged you down and let God take control. He is here, waiting for you with open arms if you but ask. "Jesus, please forgive me of all my sins. Make me clean and acceptable to God. I believe you came from Heaven and were born on this earth so that You could reveal God's love for us. By dying on the cross and shedding Your blood, You made it possible for us to be forgiven of all our sins.

Thank you Jesus. I ask for your guidance Lord to help me to know God better. In Your name I pray, Amen."

Be hopeful my dear reader, for you have just taken the first step toward salvation. God is here to comfort you and provide for all of your needs. Have faith and trust in the all knowing God who loves you dearly. I am excited for you and hope for the best for everyone who has read these words. Thank you Lord.

Lone Wolf Publishing LLC is a non-profit organization created by the author with the intent of sharing the good news of Jesus Christ and God to people struggling with addiction issues and the underserved in rehabilitation facilities or in the prison system. If you would like to support or donate, please visit and/or follow the publishing page on Facebook at:

https://www.facebook.com/lonewolfpublishing

All donations go to the distribution of books to rehab facilities or inmates in prison and also to the company for business expenses: purchase and shipment of books, purchase of ISBN's, barcodes and other organizational expenses.